{IT CHANGED THE WORLD}

INVENTION OF THE
COMBUSTION ENGINE

Mike Downs

Rourke
Educational Media

A Division of
Carson
Dellosa
Education

rourkeeducationalmedia.com

BEFORE AND DURING READING ACTIVITIES

Before Reading: *Building Background Knowledge and Vocabulary*

Building background knowledge can help children process new information and build upon what they already know. Before reading a book, it is important to tap into what children already know about the topic. This will help them develop their vocabulary and increase their reading comprehension.

Questions and Activities to Build Background Knowledge:

1. Look at the front cover of the book and read the title. What do you think this book will be about?
2. What do you already know about this topic?
3. Take a book walk and skim the pages. Look at the table of contents, photographs, captions, and bold words. Did these text features give you any information or predictions about what you will read in this book?

Vocabulary: *Vocabulary Is Key to Reading Comprehension*

Use the following directions to prompt a conversation about each word.

- Read the vocabulary words.
- What comes to mind when you see each word?
- What do you think each word means?

Vocabulary Words:

- assembly line
- aviation
- combustion
- energy
- engine
- exhaust
- gasoline
- horsepower
- piston
- textile

During Reading: *Reading for Meaning and Understanding*

To achieve deep comprehension of a book, children are encouraged to use close reading strategies. During reading, it is important to have children stop and make connections. These connections result in deeper analysis and understanding of a book.

 Close Reading a Text

During reading, have children stop and talk about the following:

- Any confusing parts
- Any unknown words
- Text to text, text to self, text to world connections
- The main idea in each chapter or heading

Encourage children to use context clues to determine the meaning of any unknown words. These strategies will help children learn to analyze the text more thoroughly as they read.

When you are finished reading this book, turn to the next-to-last page for **Text-Dependent Questions** and an **Extension Activity**.

TABLE OF CONTENTS

Engines Needed 4

Combustion with Steam 8

Internal Combustion and Automobiles 14

Farming, Flying, and More 20

Replacing Combustion 27

Glossary 30

Index 31

Text-Dependent Questions 31

Extension Activity 31

About the Author 32

ENGINES NEEDED

A fire truck roars down the street, siren blaring. It screeches to a halt in front of a burning house, and the firefighters arrive just in time! How did they get there so quickly? They relied on the **engine** inside the fire truck.

Before the **combustion** engine was invented, firefighters carried water to a fire by pulling water pumps to the location on foot. Sometimes, they used horses. Imagine how many houses burned down before firefighters could even get there. The combustion engine changed everything.

An engine is a machine that changes **energy** into work. Water wheels are some of the oldest engines. They use water energy to grind grain into flour and have to be built near flowing water.

Inventors wanted to design engines that didn't need wind, water, or animal power. The combustion engine solved this problem. Combustion engines used a wide variety of fuels and could be built in different sizes and different places.

Flowing water makes this water wheel turn. The turning parts can be used to do work such as grinding grain.

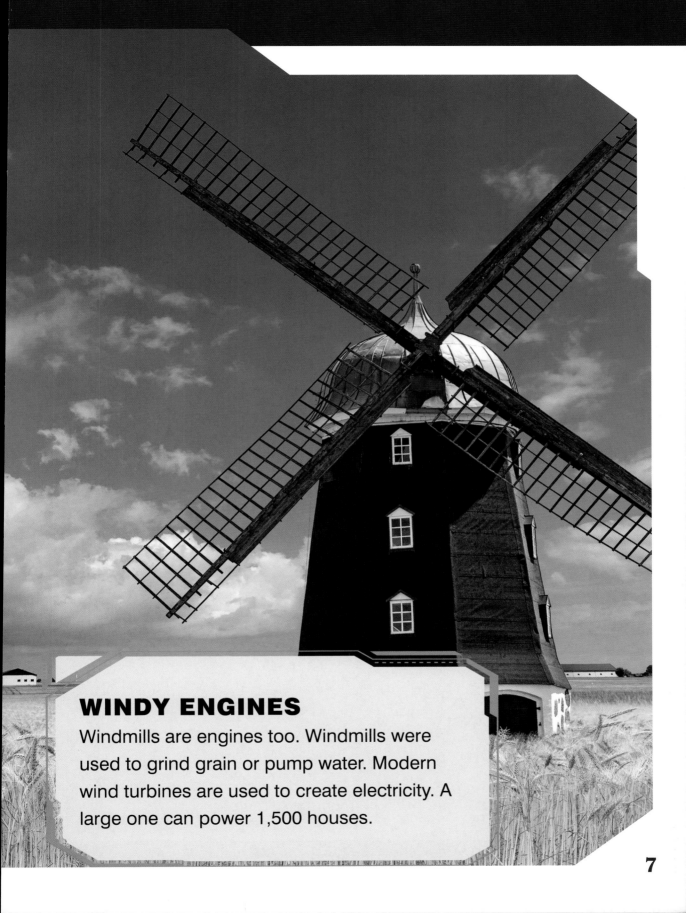

WINDY ENGINES

Windmills are engines too. Windmills were used to grind grain or pump water. Modern wind turbines are used to create electricity. A large one can power 1,500 houses.

COMBUSTION WITH STEAM

When something combusts, it explodes. Combustion engines are powered by many small explosions. The first combustion engines were steam engines. Although steam-powered devices have been used since the first century BCE, the first popular one similar to modern engines was made in 1712.

A steam engine uses heated water to create steam, and steam can move things. The lid on a pot of boiling water bounces around because of the steam energy escaping. The steam in an engine powers a pump or moves gears.

People have to load fuel into the furnace of a steam engine.

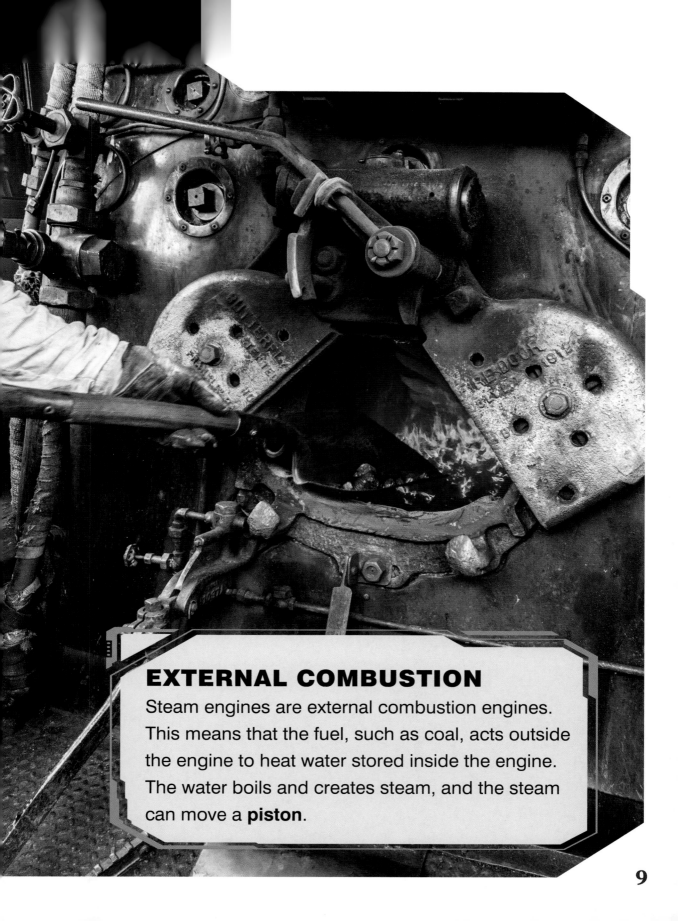

EXTERNAL COMBUSTION

Steam engines are external combustion engines. This means that the fuel, such as coal, acts outside the engine to heat water stored inside the engine. The water boils and creates steam, and the steam can move a **piston**.

Steam engines changed everything. They could be large enough to power huge factories such as **textile** mills or small enough to power vehicles. They could be built anywhere.

Steam engines in trains and boats made travel much faster. By 1890, steam-powered ocean liners crossed the Atlantic Ocean in less than a week. In contrast, this voyage took several weeks in a sailing vessel.

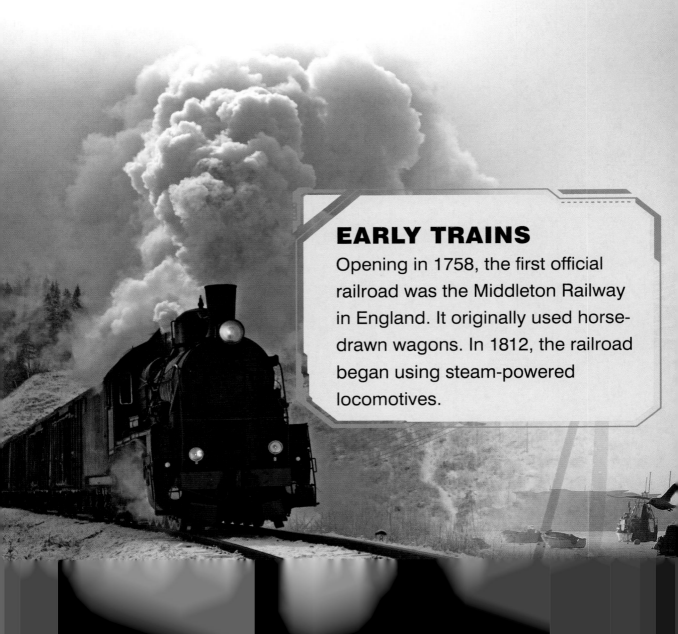

EARLY TRAINS

Opening in 1758, the first official railroad was the Middleton Railway in England. It originally used horse-drawn wagons. In 1812, the railroad began using steam-powered locomotives.

This warship was made for the Royal Navy of the United Kingdom in 1860. It was powered by steam and had 40 guns.

Steam engines had problems, however. They used a lot of fuel to do only a small amount of work and were very heavy, which made them difficult to use and repair. Some farmers tried using steam-powered tractors. These huge machines broke down easily and didn't work well on muddy farms.

In 1852, the French inventor Henri Giffard built a steam-powered airship. It had to be 144 feet (44 meters) long just to carry him and the 350-pound (160-kilogram) engine. The engine produced only three **horsepower**, which is about the same amount of power produced by a modern lawn mower engine.

THE REAL MCCOY

The inventor Elijah McCoy patented more than 40 devices that improved steam engine maintenance. Most of them automatically added oil to steam engines. Many machines could work longer and better using his inventions.

Giffard's steam-powered airship was tied down before it was launched.

INTERNAL COMBUSTION AND AUTOMOBILES

Inventors wanted to design smaller, more powerful engines, but that would require a different type of fuel: **gasoline**. Gasoline burns more efficiently than wood or coal. The use of gasoline as a fuel led to the invention of the internal combustion engine.

Internal combustion engines could be very small, and they would eventually power hundreds of new inventions. Automobiles were one of those inventions. These machines changed the world.

INTERNAL COMBUSTION ENGINES: HOW THEY WORK

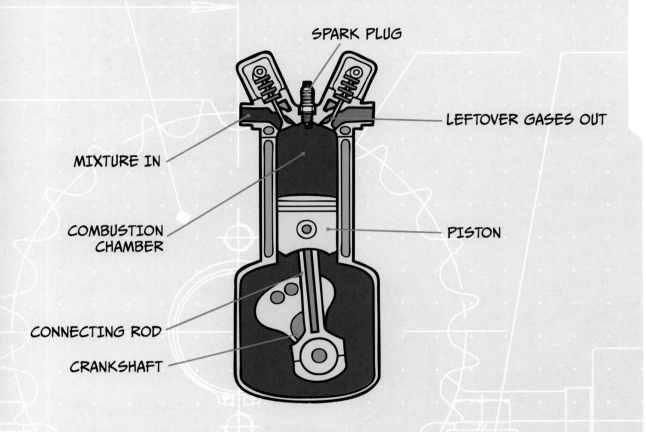

SPARK PLUG

LEFTOVER GASES OUT

MIXTURE IN

PISTON

COMBUSTION CHAMBER

CONNECTING ROD

CRANKSHAFT

INTERNAL COMBUSTION

Internal combustion engines burn fuel inside hollow cylinders. The air in the cylinders is compressed by a piston. Fuel is squirted into the engine, and a spark plug ignites the fuel. The mixture explodes, moving the piston and making the crankshaft turn.

Not everyone thought automobiles were a good idea. Early versions of automobiles, called horseless carriages, were noisy and sometimes unreliable. Even Siegfried Marcus, who invented one of the first gasoline-powered cars, didn't like them. He called the automobile a "senseless waste of time and energy."

By 1910, though, automobiles had become increasingly popular. People who could afford them started using cars instead of walking or using horses for travel. Some car owners even began taking long drives to visit new places.

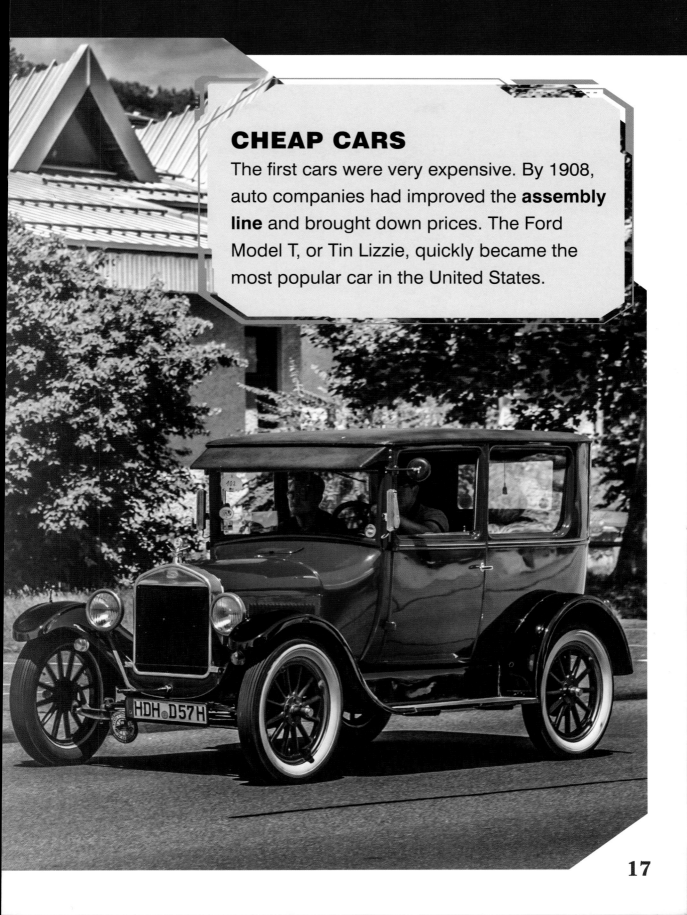

CHEAP CARS

The first cars were very expensive. By 1908, auto companies had improved the **assembly line** and brought down prices. The Ford Model T, or Tin Lizzie, quickly became the most popular car in the United States.

Automobiles eventually changed transportation worldwide. Before 1900, only a few thousand cars were sold around the world. In 2018, about 80 million cars were sold. That's enough cars, bumper-to-bumper, to encircle Earth almost 10 times!

As combustion engines improved and cars became more common, auto racing became a popular hobby. In 1895, the winner of a Paris-to-Bordeaux race in France averaged 15 miles (24 kilometers) per hour. Racers today can drive much faster.

SPEEDING UP

A few winners at the Indianapolis 500, a famous car race, have averaged over 180 miles (290 kilometers) per hour. They achieve these fast speeds with highly advanced engines in cars doing laps on an oval track.

FARMING, FLYING, AND MORE

Combustion engines soon were used to drive farm equipment. Powerful tractors could pull tillers, spreaders, mowers, and other machines behind them. Huge combines could cut, thresh, and clean grain at the same time.

This amazing increase in productivity changed farming forever. In 1900, it took nearly 40 hours of labor to produce 100 bushels of corn. Using machines with combustion engines, the same work could be done with less than three hours of labor.

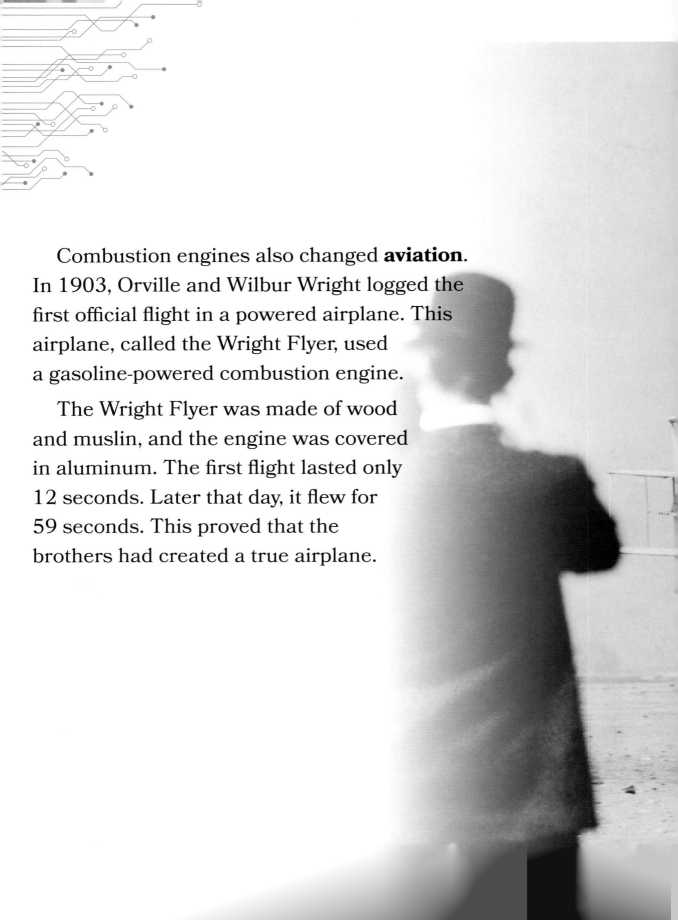

Combustion engines also changed **aviation**. In 1903, Orville and Wilbur Wright logged the first official flight in a powered airplane. This airplane, called the Wright Flyer, used a gasoline-powered combustion engine.

The Wright Flyer was made of wood and muslin, and the engine was covered in aluminum. The first flight lasted only 12 seconds. Later that day, it flew for 59 seconds. This proved that the brothers had created a true airplane.

Powered airplanes massively changed both warfare and tourism. In war, airplanes were used as bombers, fighters, transports, and spy planes. The ability of planes to quickly fly passengers to faraway destinations changed how people traveled for pleasure and work.

Combustion engines weren't limited to big machines. Inventors and manufacturers developed smaller engines, which led to an explosion of new products. Lawn mowers, scooters, generators, motor boats, and go-karts are only a few examples.

Consider a typical lawn service. The owner drives a truck. They have a lawnmower, an edger, a string trimmer, and a leaf blower. All of those tools might be used to mow and trim a lawn. That's a total of five combustion engines used for just one task.

Millions of machines use combustion engines. Hundreds of thousands of jobs have been created as a result of this one invention and all of the changes it has inspired. In 2020, the global market for combustion engines will be more than 200 billion dollars.

REPLACING COMBUSTION

But combustion engines have problems. They are noisy, and they emit **exhaust**. Exhaust causes smog in cities and contributes to acid rain and global warming. Global warming, in turn, leads to rising seas, flooding, and increased droughts and wildfires.

Combustion engines also need gasoline. To make gasoline, oil has to be pumped from underground. This can damage the environment. The 2010 *Deepwater Horizon* oil spill dumped almost 3.2 billion gallons of oil into the Gulf of Mexico. Another big problem is that Earth's supply of oil is limited.

The combustion engine has powered the world for more than a century. What's next? Cleaner and quieter electric engines are now replacing some combustion engines. Perhaps you will become famous for inventing a new kind of engine that powers the world for the next hundred years.

ELECTRIC FUTURE

Automobile makers around the world are introducing electric cars. Forecasts expect electric car sales to be 10 times higher by 2025. China leads the way, selling 579,000 electric and hybrid cars in 2017.

An oil rig, at left, pumps oil from under the ocean. Here, a person drives an all-electric car that produces no exhaust.

GLOSSARY

assembly line (uh-SEM-blee line): a production method in which many workers stay in one spot doing a single job as the product, such as a car, moves from one worker to another

aviation (ay-vee-AY-shuhn): the making, design, and use of airplanes or other flying machines

combustion (kuhm-BUS-chuhn): related to the act of burning something

energy (EN-ur-jee): the power from wind, water, or any fuel that can be used to do work

engine (ehn-JIN): a machine that converts energy into mechanical force and motion

exhaust (ig-ZAWST): the leftover gases discharged from an engine

gasoline (gas-uh-LEEN): a fuel made from oil

horsepower (HORS-pow-ur): a unit for measuring the power of an engine; originally, the work output of one horse

piston (PIS-tuhn): the part of an internal combustion engine that moves back and forth in the cylinder

textile (TEK-stile): related to cloth or material made by weaving

INDEX

automobile 14

boats 10

coal 9, 14

external combustion engine 9

global warming 27

internal combustion engine
  14, 15

invention(s) 12, 14, 16

locomotive 10

machine(s) 6, 12, 14, 20,
  24, 26

steam 8, 9, 10, 12, 13

TEXT-DEPENDENT QUESTIONS

1. What was the first type of combustion engine?
2. What types of transportation use combustion engines?
3. What are some problems with combustion engines?
4. How do combustion engines affect your everyday life?
5. How have speeds in auto racing changed over the years?

EXTENSION ACTIVITY

The combustion engine led to huge changes in transportation. Design a new kind of engine. How is it powered? What is important in your design? How could it be used? Draw your engine and two ways that it could be used.

ABOUT THE AUTHOR

Combustion engines allowed Mike Downs to learn how to fly! Now he flies a combustion-powered Pawnee airplane, but mostly he flies jets. He also loves to write and go on adventures. His next adventure will be learning to fly a powered paraglider with a small combustion engine on his back.

www.rourkeeducationalmedia.com

PHOTO CREDIT: Cover: ©Marco_Bonfanti; pages 4-5: ©JT Vintage / Glasshouse Images; page 6: ©Milkovasa; page 7: ©Agaten; pages 8-9: ©Christopher Badzioch; page 10: ©yomoyo; page 11: ©Max Speed: pages 12-13, 16b: ©LOC; page 12: ©Wiki; page 15: ©Monkik; page 16a, 22-23: ©Everett Historical; page 17: ©Gaschwald; page 18-19: ©Justin R. Noe ASP; page 20-21: ©ArtistGNDphotography; page 24: ©TomSmith585; page 25: ©Cbradovic; page 26: ©Tramino; page 27: ©milehightraveler; page 28: ©nielubieklonv; page 29: ©Sjo

Edited by: Tracie Santos
Cover and interior layout by: Kathy Walsh

Library of Congress PCN Data

Invention of the Combustion Engine / Mike Downs
(It Changed the World)
ISBN 978-1-73162-984-5 (hard cover)(alk. paper)
ISBN 978-1-73162-978-4 (soft cover)
ISBN 978-1-73162-990-6 (e-Book)
ISBN 978-1-73163-337-8 (ePub)
Library of Congress Control Number: 2019945510

Rourke Educational Media
Printed in the United States of America,
North Mankato, Minnesota